FORGE

FORGE
Jan Zwicky

GASPEREAU PRESS MMXI

Take me to the place where I can climb no further.
Leave me barefoot in the snow and mapless:
I will come to you. Marry someone else, raise children:
I will sleep each night, my shoulder
to the weather-stripping of your basement door.
Join the Foreign Legion, sell the farm,
change your name and work the night shift at the HoJo:
I'll remember. Throw it away:
I'll find it. Throw it away and I will carry it,
dented, smudged and shining. In your greatest joy,
I will be the light before you. In your grief,
the air demanding entrance to your lungs.
Die, and I will be the fire you lie in.
I will be the fire you made because you loved.

MUSIC AND SILENCE:
SEVEN VARIATIONS

I

Who can name the absence
music is, who draw that space,
the cold breath, sudden and empty
that will own you the rest of your life?

In the still light, you put your feet down,
this one, that one, then this one,
again on the yellow earth. Your happiness
was like the trees': golden and tattered.

Who could you have told? Leaves
fell around you, half shrug, half sorrow.
And the wind sprang up off the water
riding you, fierce, unbiddable, already lost.

II

In secret, you have hoped that it might
come into your hand. No wonder
you're afraid: you could be blinded
by the air's transparence, made meltwater

by a single wayward breeze.
Already it has made you homeless, already
taken your name: and this
without touching you. In your dream,

laughter, a hallway, ordinary daylight,
you are turning.... And then? Move a muscle,
you will fall. Breathe
and there will be no other breath.

III

Tears; confusion; and more tears.
Is it possible for clamour to become a life?
You negotiate the news like a bad canoeist,
voices shouting, shouting from the rapids.

Yet always the fragrance of that glance,
the thought you could be, still,
adrift among the willows.
Each day, a plan becomes less likely.

You leave work early or forget to go.
Memory opens in you like an undereye,
your hand dissolving in its amber shafts:
dark dream in which you cannot find your way.

IV

The pool stretched from the shallow steps behind the house.
You hadn't noticed until after you arrived
that it was dusk. And how the land on all sides
dropped away: miles to the valley floor.

The figure stepped out from your body,
arced above the surface, dove.
You might have stood forever, silence
shawling through the air like snow.

Crystal: blue: lit somewhere
from inside its depths. Even then
you didn't want to understand.
Even then, you knew.

v

All day, the winter light comes striding
down the strait and through the window.
Golden, thick with silence, and you
not knowing how to walk or speak.

This is your perplexity:
was it a hand
that reached up, plucked the arrow
in mid-flight? Or were you all along

arriving here, sidelong, failed,
but currented? A reason
would release you: this is how you know
it won't be found.

VI

But no figure steps before you now.
You're paralyzed by hope, the thought
you haven't understood. Your hand is trembling
as it moves to lift the latch.

Would it be better if that voice
had never spoken? —The still flight in your chest,
the echo of that glance.
What answer can you give?

The clouds pace over you, the bright wind
old, wanting to be finished.
Your resolve is clumsy with grief.
Every step you take is in the wrong direction.

VII

That sound: something in you has been ringing ever since.
And you, stumbling at the edges of your self,
deaf, bewildered. Was it joy?
You were smaller than dust, dumb

as pebbles. Yes, you'd hoped your throat
would fill, your lungs. But you were
emptier than winter, defenceless.
You could not even tell yourself. And it was then

the flame inside you stood straight up,
tall, gold-coloured; and your heart walked forward
easily, as though something had called it, laid itself
on the anvil of that silence.

LATE SCHUBERT

A warm night in autumn, summery,
lying on the bed upstairs, a dog
barking somewhere in the distance: you are thinking
of your childhood, your long-dead father, or not
thinking so much as letting them
nudge up against you, boats
moored at the same dock on a still night, and a wavelet
made by who knows what wake, what storm, lifts them gently,
      briefly,
together, air glassy with calm, the moon
staring down. Isn't love
always like this? —A spider's thread, spindrift
with the tensile strength of steel. The light must fall
just so to make it visible, faint gleam
twisting above you, pulling
from so deep, so far back, you think it must be anchored
some place before you were born.
                      And the fever,
the restlessness, the way the heart surges
against the breakwater, plunges,
and surges again: isn't this
the same thing? —Love
afraid it won't get home, afraid
it will forget. Is dying
that hard? Its horizon

is the same shape as your life — wild hillsides
pointing to the wind, the sea
heaving under the sky's emptiness.

                          Let your hand
move into that darkness above your face: almost
you can feel the stars —

                    their silence,
steady on the other side.

KINDERSZENEN

after Robert Schumann, Op. 15

Snowcrust after freezing rain, the cool, lost clarity
in the light. And the long field gathering shadows
the way the heart once gathered hope —
willow-tendrils and the massy tangle of the aspens,
the hay bales, even you — stretched,
blurred and luminous, across the unmarked snow.

Is it their weightlessness that makes them seem
like memory? The starched tablecloths,
the pinafores, someone laughing in the dim spruce-filtered
       light, air resinous
with love. Or do we call it memory
because we cannot bear to say
the longed-for that did not come to pass.
To find, this late, the distances inside oneself
uncrossable. The riddle
of forgiveness.

The red in the willows like forgotten laughter.
The weightless snow-blue of that glance.
How long the shadows are.
How long the heart is.

OUT WALKING, THINKING ABOUT
THE SOUND OF THE VIOL

It's a blue sky today, ice
on the step. In the woods,
the beech tree is turning: two branches,
the rest still green. Its leaves
are stiff and supple, a fine
starched leather, more burnt
than tanned. What amazes most,
though, is the colour: its evenness
uncanny; shy, sinewy, a shade
our mothers might deem
serviceable in a shirt or coat, in isolation
unremarkable. Yet leaf against leaf,
branch on branch, that spare bronze
flares: voiceless
and articulate, clean
spoken through.

SITTING OUTSIDE AFTER LUNCH,
READING, IN MY FIFTIETH YEAR

At the other end of the porch, sudden commotion
in the bamboos: sharp breeze
from nowhere, the turn from fore to after noon
tousling the pages of my book some seconds later,
once the leaves fall still.
                                    How easily
I might have missed it, caught in
heat's silence, as I was: I catch myself
head lifted, taken
by surprise by sound.

RUNNING ERRANDS, CATCHING
SIGHT OF MY REFLECTION

Turning that corner,
no warning, the face
in the plate glass
startles me: not
beautiful, not ugly, but
familiar somehow: someone
I might want
to get to know. My self, too,
in that moment, no more
than a foot or hand: useful,
unabashed,
pulling on its glove.

NIGHT MUSIC

You remember it as winter, but what you see
are leaf-shadows on the cupboard door,
black in the moonlight,
shifting a little in some breeze,
then still.

3:00 a.m., barefoot in the kitchen,
moon-shadows of the lilac on the cupboard door,
gathered with you on the threshold.

You are only trying to say
what you see in the world. Spring.
Winter. Even knowing what you love
is no salvation. Their heart shapes,
trembling in the moonlight, sharp as frost.

NOJACK

He said he'd meet her at the Mohawk,
hoped she didn't mind, he had stuff stored out that way
he needed to pick up, and she just wanting to drive
somewhere, to be driven, without thought —
December, the day bright, mild,
they needed only sweaters,
and she'd lost her gloves.
What is it a woman can do for a man,
his grief so deep it's colourless, like sunlight —
her own deeper. How she made him stop
and scooped snow from the ditch
to clean the windshield. His surprise.
Or later, her body nearly weightless across his,
head in the hollow of his shoulder:
the distance of it. Where were they going
anyway, that day? Sundogs
brilliant to the south, meltwater
sheeting the highway, poplars, black spruce
jutting from the far ridge and beyond them
the solstice slowly filling the horizon: purple, orange,
pink, cream, blue, turquoise,
white.

SMALL SONG ON SURRENDER

Overcast: the day ends
turning inward, no last thoughts.
A way of letting go
without regrets,
cold catching at the hem of my skirt.
But the way you caught my hand....

There will also come a first time:
your touch, naming something in me
so new it will have no depth:
sky on a windless, snowy night,
its ceaseless self-erasure, that endless
tender sifting of the dark.

LYING DOWN IN MY HOTEL ROOM, THINKING ABOUT THE DAY

I have spent too long
telling the world the world is the world
and poetry is made of language.
Today on the Bedford platform, I began
the great poem: weeping openly on the public
telephone — the way some were staring
as they swirled past, the way some
weren't — yes: it was the truth
at last.

PRACTISING BACH

for performance with Bach's E Major
Partita for Solo Violin, BWV 1006

PRELUDE

There is, said Pythagoras, a sound
the planet makes: a kind of music
just outside our hearing, the proportion
and the resonance of things — not
the clang of theory or the wuthering
of human speech, not even
the bright song of sex or hunger, but
the unrung ringing that
supports them all.

The wife, no warning, dead
when you come home. Ducats
in the fishheads that you salvage
from the rubbish heap. Is the cosmos
laughing at us? No. It's saying

improvise. Everywhere you look
there's beauty, and it's rimed
with death. If you find injustice
you'll find humans, and this means
that if you listen, you'll find love.
The substance of the world is light,
is water: here, clear
even when it's dying; even when the dying
seems unbearable, it runs.

LOURE

Why is Bach's music more like speech than any other? Because
of its wisdom, I think. Which means its tempering of lyric
passion by domesticity, its grounding of the flash of lyric
insight in domestic earth, the turf of dailiness.

Let us think of music as a geometry of the emotions.
Bach's practice, then, resembles that of the Egyptians: earth's
measure as a way of charting the bottomlands of the Nile,
the floodwaters of the heart, as a way of charting life. Opera,
Greek tragedy, Romantic poetry tell us that sex and death are
what we have to focus on if we want to understand any of the
rest. Bach's music, by contrast, speaks directly to, and of, life
itself — the resonant ground of sex and death.

And it does this not without ornamentation, but
without fuss: the golden ratio in the whelk shell lying on
the beach, the leaf whorl opening to sun, the presence of the
divine in the chipped dish drying in the rack, *that* miracle:
good days, bad days, a sick kid, a shaft of sunlight on the organ
bench. *Talk to me, I'm listening.*

GAVOTTE

E major: June wind
in the buttercups, wild
and bright and tough.
Like luck — a truth
that's on the surface of a thing,
not because it's shallow, but because
it's open: overtoned.
Because it rings.
                    Fate, too,
is character. But it's
the shape — the cadence
and the counterpoint. Luck
lives in the moment, and it
looks at you: the clear eye,
gold, when being sings.

MENUET I & II

There's nothing special in it. All you have to do
is hit the right key at the right time. Time:
that stream in which we do, and do not,
live. *Just practise diligently; it will all go well. You have*
five fingers on each hand, each one as healthy as my own.
Unison, the octave; the fifth, the fourth, the third.
Of the strings? The viola, if I have a choice.
At the keyboard, don't forget to use your thumb.
God's glory and the recreation of the mind.
What I really need to know:
does the organ have good lungs?
The partita of the world, the dance of being: *everything*
has to be possible.

BOURÉE

Partita, partie — a whole of many parts. Pythagoras, who is said to have studied with the Egyptians, is also said to have taught that enlightenment meant solving the problem of the One and the Many, of coming to grasp the divine unity of the world through its bits and pieces, as these come to us in language.

This may also be thought of as the problem of metaphor: that metaphor's truth, its charge of meaning, depends on the assertion of identity and difference, on erotic coherence and referential strife, on meaning as resonance and meaning revealed through analysis.

Lyric poets are always trying to approach the issue by forcing speech to aspire to the condition of music. Bach comes at it from the other end: he infuses music with a sense of the terrible concreteness, the particularity, of the world. And enlightenment? —Acceptance of, delight in, the mystery of incarnation.

GIGUE

    There is a sound
that is a whole of many parts,
a sorrowless transparency, like luck,
that opens in the centre of a thing.
An eye, a river, fishheads, death,
gold in your pocket, and a half-wit
son: the substance of the world
is light and blindness and the measure
of our wisdom is our love.
Our diligence: ten fingers and
a healthy set of lungs. Practise
ceaselessly: there is
one art: wind
in the open spaces
grieving, laughing
with us, saying
improvise.

YOUR GAZE

I step in, out of the century,
to the calm light of your eyes.
Here, each thing is itself — as though
a vault, reaching into darkness,
held back a weight so we could breathe.

It shines, your grey gaze,
shines. And I lean
into that silence, the world that opens now
against the long draw of your body. The arc
it draws through me.

GEMINI

*after J. S. Bach, Cello Suite No. 5 in
C Minor, BWV 1011, Sarabande*

There is a life
in which I do not find you.

Handedness that does not know
it's paired, a voice
that does not recognize
its line as counterpoint.

As though I were to learn
the air through which I'd grown
had not been fluid, making room
for me, but that my life
had curled and trellised on
some absent shape of emptiness
that had the shape of you.

The stories of Stickwalking
God, or One-Side: half a man,
one leg, one arm. And yet
he is a marksman
and a hunter. Spear points. Tips.

His half a heart and
its unbroken love. They say
it leaps out from his side
each time it beats.

VESPERS

A closed door, its long
quiet window. All day

the light's slow drift
across the mountains:

snow: the distant gleam
of the life I have lost.

All night, your kiss: its
dark petals, my slow unfolding

under it. You
walk towards me

out of that mystery:
the death that's yet to come.

SARABANDE

after J. S. Bach, Cello Suite No. 6 in D Major, BWV 1012

A dance for firelight, candlelight, the time of day
a lamp might be turned low — the muscle in it
like a banked fire, and its sweetness like the muscle in
your breast, your forearm, the fragility, just here,
above your brow. And what this speaks of:
a tenderness we cannot teach perhaps
until we die — that leaving from which
there is no return. The long emptiness,
made sharp, acute, by memory, the emptiness
that is the definition of this music — everywhere
your eyes, your tongue, your hands — its outline
in the darkness that it presses up against.
                                        The dead
are with us always, talking to us while we work
and in our sleep — but this, this
is the language of what lives: hold me,
beloved of the slow dance, beloved of the long allemande,
hold me, rib, breastbone, shoulder, eye
that holds my eye. Dance of the earth
that drinks rain through us, of the sky that drinks
the earth through rain, teach me, bright centre of
the long silence, these steps, notes, chords
that I will never finish learning,
this life, which is my life.

PURCELL: FANTASIA FOR FIVE VIOLS, "UPON ONE NOTE"

As in autumn, the great flame
descends, stepping down into the world.
The slow flame, stepping down.
Great shelves of light
laid out along the rock and ripeness
in the green heat of the forest,
in the gold heat of the fields.
The flame steps down; the story
once again unfolds. The burning
that is never done is
consummation — the taking whole
of joy, the willing
immolation of the green breath on the altar
of the blue transparent air.
And with each step,
from the beginning, something
climbing: steady, calm, like
hope, but deeper,
made of earth. Fidelity. Which lifts,
unfolding, emptied, in the rain
of light, the stepping down around it
of its dissolution, beauty more
than any of us can bear. Which is
gratitude for brokenness, its arms
raised to the emerald scattering

of leaves. O, let there be
fleet clouds, the clatter of the doves
like bright seed, laughter. Let there be
grief, green as dew-wet moss at dawn.
The world steps on its way. The earth
under its light, all praise, all sorrow,
ripening. It is. It knows.
It carries you.

TRANSIT

So it was: your hand went willingly
towards the latch. You stepped out
into twilight, splay of cloud against the west's
last light, that shadowland
where we are least afraid,

where our blindness is complete.
Did you feel it then,
those lips against your cheek, that breath
dissolving in your hair? It rose before you,
placed the cool wisp of its palm above your heart

and you were caught, split,
held: the farthest rooms in you flung open.
And its voice reached up into the night, then,
and the god, slick, dripping,
stepped out from the darkness. Entered you.

IF THERE WERE TWO RIVERS

If there were two rivers.
If their water were clear gold.
If it were a flood, a homecoming, and where they joined,
      a standing wave, its crest of white.
If you climbed the hill alone, returning,
      and the grass was golden in the evening light.
If the golden water leaked around your feet
      out of the earth.
If it was everywhere you stepped — gold, streaming,
      and the clear light going down.
If, in the other dream, the children ran away.

If it were a ship, and the evening light at sea.
If it were a church, and the orange light of evening.
If there were no roof or walls.
If it was made of fire.
If it were radiant.
If it were massive, weightless, and a white fire
      misting from its centre like a breath.
If the rock was raw but glistening.
If it lit the foyer — if the light were all below and
      the other rooms were dusk.
If what happened was: you stood there.
If there was nothing to be said.

If it glowed.
If the glow was like a silent speech.
If the light was like a haze, a mist: if every detail
          were exact.
If it broke you open.
If your blood shone on the hearth.
If the silence deafened you.
If what you saw was the necessity.
If the hammer of it brought you to your knees.
If the hammer of it clove your heart.

If what lay below was light.
If what you could not find was there.
If its hard fire was a golden river.
If the golden river was a forge.
If the forge was rock, and if the rock was shining.
If the forge was love.

FROM DISTANT LANDS

after Robert Schumann, Kinderszenen, Op. 15

Or was it a gust of wind? I had been walking
as I always walked, along that hallway, a place
I'd passed each day for years and never noticed,
thinking about summer, thinking
about sunlight, the anonymity of love: and then
you touched me — did you touch me? —
and the door I'd never seen swung back, flew open
and the wind that swept its hand across my face
passed by.
           And on the other side — the plain wood
of that casing, the simple latch — not
an attic, not a cloakroom, but
a castle: oak and glass and polished stone.
It was caverned, glistening, windows
with the loft of mountain air and floors
like northern lakes at twilight: I stepped in, didn't think
to see if you had followed, silence
pulling, shimmering, down corridors, through
walls. But when at last I turned and called, the echo
told me.
        Like the moonlight
drifting in those never-furnished rooms.

YOUR EYES

Like the hot clear light that flares
along the loft door's unstopped edge:
your eyes, each morning,
opening.

      Or dim, loft-dark themselves,
sea-grey and cloudy,
bruised with love.

          Or like the wave tip,
sharpening in thought, dissolving
in the instant of its grasp
to spume:

      the soul made visible
as the body breaks.

ADMETOS

after Rilke's "Alkestis"

He wakes
sometimes in the night and wonders
if she has woken too, and then
remembers.
            The body that's beside him
stirs, hair lank with sweat, whuffs,
settles. And the fury
starts to fist in him again, so that
he almost turns to press his stiffness
up against that warmth, but sometimes, in the dark, he'll smell
the silence, or the rain, and then, like music
that he can't quite hear, the grief under the fury
tugs, the way joy did
the second when the god first smiled, so that
he stands there on the brink once more,
his childhood in his mouth, his hundred changeless lives a line
of mirrored ghosts behind him, something
lifting, lifting at the centre of him, poised
above the bed where transformation was refused, and then
the terror, and the falling back, the cold sick
of it, and he turns, the image of
her arm outstretched, the hand that almost reached him,
drives himself into the sudden flesh,
blind, hard.

WHEN YOU LOOK UP

When you look up, or out,
or in, your seeing is
a substance: stuff: a density
of some kind, like a pitch
that's just outside the range
of hearing: numb
nudge of the real.
                              I saw air
once, in its nothingness
so clear it was a voice
almost, a kind of joy. I thought
of water — breath as drinking —
and the way it shows us
light. Or maybe it was light
I thought of — as though
water were the solid form
of wind, and air
a language with a single word
transparent to the world.
Your glance is this,
meltwater, mountain light.
The plunge and thunder of the pool.
The ripple at its farthest edge.

DIOTIMA TO HÖLDERLIN:
A REMONSTRANCE

Διανοῇ οὖν δεινός ποτε γενήσεσθαι τὰ ἐρωτικά,
ἐὰν ταῦτα μὴ ἐννοῇς; SYMPOSIUM 207C

All of you, your pricks in the air,
wishing you were dead. It's true
that asked or unasked,
the god comes, true
that patriarchy, capital, and even simple loyalty,
must find this difficult.
But if you crucify desire,
you build inside yourself the wall
from which you'll hang the body of the world.
If eros clouds your vision,
look into the cloud. The earth, the golden lilies,
do not want your pain —
they do not believe in any of the names
you wish it had. To see,
you must become the thing
you do not want:
invisible to history, invisible
to other men. You must find
the blind spot of the dad who never loved you
anyway — the one you sometimes met
out in his chariot, or on the staircase

heading upstairs with your mom — and dump
the hemlock. Just step here,
barefoot in sunlight. Take your shoes off,
step here — not
above the brook, but in.
Dissolve the nothingness you are
by walking into it. Epiktetos,
who'd been a slave, knew how. You've seen
some women do it. Love.

SONG OF FAREWELL

for RMA in memoriam

Beloved, I am anxious to be off.
The snow has come to the high passes
and my life is light within me.
The seed has burst and spills before the wind.

Beloved, it is time to put aside the words of love.
You, who could not bear love's terror,
must let go. The stalk that will not break
cannot be harvested.

Love, beloved, hollowed out my heart.
It took my eyes, my hands, my voice
and left me glad. Sorrow
buried them beneath the gateway where you stood.

Until you find the self
you cannot give the self away.
Search hard that you might follow me,
beloved: I am gone.

THE ART OF FUGUE

I

A room, a table, and four chairs.
The chairs are made of wood,
the floor is wood,
the walls are bare. But windowed.
West light, east light. And a scent
like cedar in the air. Here, the self
will sit down with the self.
Now it will say
what it has to say. It looks
into its own eyes. Listens.

11

A table, four chairs, east light,
west. This is your self:
what's left
when it has been forgiven
by itself, when it
forgives. You feel it — it's
the weight of breath,
transparent, clear.
It folds its hands,
looks up at you. You listen.

III

The self. They've told you
that there's no such thing. A truth.
But one of many. Come
from the other side, from underneath
erasure, chew your way through light toward
different intelligence: you find
that something, even in the task of letting go,
goes on, has been; and in the cold shock of the plunge,
your feet touch bottom. Sound
comes out of silence, is
its inner sense. The river of your
listening, and the river of your voice.

West light, east light, a wooden table
and four chairs: multiple, multiple, multiple
are the voices of the inmost heart.
Sister, brother, husband, wife.
Father, mother, daughter, son.
The compass points of human being
and the being of red alder and
the black-tailed deer. Sleep and hunger,
hope and loss. Silence,
and the bar of sunlight on the floor.

V

Sleep and hunger.
Hope and loss.
Sister, brother,
mother, son.
The floorboards of the soul
are birth, are death,
the four-eyed love
that makes a child.
The patterns in your life
repeat themselves
as premonitions, sudden gifts.
A scent like cedar
drifting in the room. A table
and four chairs.

VI

Once again, the moment of impossible
transition, the bow, its silent voice
above the string. Let us say
the story goes like this. Let us say
you could start anywhere.
Let us say you took your splintered being
by the hand, and led it
to the centre of a room: starlight
through the floorboards of the soul.
The patterns of your life
repeat themselves until you listen.
Forgive this. Say now
what you have to say.

VII

The dead are dead:
parents, siblings, children, spouse.
Death comes upon us:
blindness, deafness, madness, or
the slow gag of neglect.
Put your arms around them:
they are what is given, as you knew.
Hand takes hand.
Dave Dravecky: cancer of the elbow.
Sigmund Freud: cancer of the mouth.
The man who had a heart attack,
and who survived,
because he fell in love.
Your own death, lifting from your past
to meet you: palmprints multiple and
shaped to match your own.

VIII

So it begins. Silence
gathers, looks up, and becomes
a voice: the thrum, the distillate,
we call a soul. Impossible
translation, for the breath
that moves in you
is wind, the wind
that cherishes the trees and cools
the stars. You are,
you are not,
nothing, shaped
by what you love. The echo
of what's left when everything
has been let go.

IX

A voice from the other side, a river: here,
the current steady, there, thickened with silt —
shoals, sandbars, the spill of grief, misunderstanding,
hope and love. You've come
to it before, birdwatching maybe,
looking mostly at the trees. But
now you know. Now you will set
the suitcase down, the backpack, and the book
you love, the book you haven't read, your lunch.
The water's neither cold nor warm.
Your mind has never been as clear.

x

Once again, the moment of impossible
translation: how good it is
the heart has settled out its load
of wanting and regret. To take
what's left and lead it to the centre of the room —
a table, four chairs, and the river
of the human voice. The floorboards
have been swept, the room
is bare, square to the compass of
your death and birth. You fold
your hands, look up — it's
nothing: light
ahead of you —

AUTOBIOGRAPHY

In the years when winter snow piled up
along the edges of the streets, beneath the windows,
on the lee side of the hedge,
I did my homework at a desk my father built,
set in the corner of my bedroom, facing west.
Which was my choice, I think. The second desk,
I know it was. And once I moved out, the apartments
with the bad floors and the crazy plumbing,
the wallpaper I was always steaming off, I'd take
the place because it had a workspace
that did not face east.

Those cold bright years.
How long I spent, trying to die.

Such injustice. When every morning
it's spring again. Every morning
the light melts the snow —
before books, before desks, before windows,
before pain, before amazement.

LOVE SONG

Your weight now
becomes my own. Your eye,
which is fire, which is sleep.

A door opens: gold light
from another life. O,

this unfolding into birdsong,
into leaves! O,

the lilt of you.

AUTUMN AGAIN

for Don McKay

Late August at my window: the restlessness
in the dying grass, no longer drawn by light
but only air, the light itself — unflexed,
the fluid stretch of summer done —
moving inside itself, unseeing.
                              All day
the crickets chanting, bright glitter on the surface
of the ebb. And ravens
talking to themselves, the flocks
of chickadees. What is
human happiness? Last night, the broad leaves
of the grass at dusk fell still, the stillness
falling through them, breathing out
its heft of dew. I stood a long time at the window
listening: crickets in the darkness,
chanting, chanting.

CROSSING THE DEZADEASH,
HAINES JUNCTION

It comes to you often in the moments
that you have alone: perhaps you've died.
Climbing the stairs between offices,
you've noticed it, a slowing of perception, a
slightly altered angle of
attack, the smell, for example, of the plastic sealant
in the windows, heating in the sun. It would be,
you think, the reason
that you seem to care so little, why you take
such risks. Or now,
the highway, no deadline, the shafts
of sun, dark drifts of cloud —
it's new, this spaciousness, this not
thinking dying would be easier. The ice
has just come off, and the five feet
of packed, wet snow: the branch
they pressed into the sand and gravel:
lift it. How that hollow feels,
shining damply. How,
even though the snow is gone, and the stick,
it keeps its shape. Look up:
old ice in the high light:
a torch, a sword,
speaking.

SMALL SONG

When you kiss me, snow is falling.
It fills the pine trees in the night.
My grief slips from me like a shawl then,
like lace. Your hands
lift the pins from my hair.

SMALL SONG: FALLING ASLEEP

In the dark, the slow surf of your breathing,
its erosion of my night fears, of the day fears
I have carried with me into night.

In the twilight, earlier, your shoulder
gold above me like the earth, and now
beneath my head, it's sky —

that field of ancient starlight, end
and opening, landfall inside falling,
unnamed reach along the shore of sight.

AND THIS

Faint haze of green, like fever
in the poplars by the draw;
their scent, raw, dizzied, where the leaf-tip
splits the bud; and the headlong rush of new grass
under wind, dark waves
rising on the hillside in the naked light.
And this, that breaks inside me: you.

SCHUMANN: FANTASIE, OP. 17

Everything already lost: this always
is the moment where we must begin.
Ecstasy: the self's ghost
standing where you left it, paralyzed,
aghast, and joy, praise,
flooding your lips, your fingertips, the voice in you
huge and exquisite, its mouth
on the nape of your neck.

The west light, the north storm,
to have known, not to have known:
because that touch was silence
and the body is your home,

you will be named,
you will be seen,
the wing will open in you,
breaking. You,
caught in the slipstream of
your own bright anonymity,
you will be spoken to,
stunned, helpless, the wave rising through you
in the dark. Don't
pull the curtain: let the black pane
see you: you,
in the mouth of the night.

Not knowing, knowing:
each worse, each holding
decades in its hand: kitchens,
dumb jokes, kindness and the shine
on the knob of the gearshift in the February sun.
If there were a sword, a block, you think
you'd lay your head along that coolness,
close your eyes. But no,
the blood springs elsewhere, touch
flooding you with silence. You are born
and born again into your life.

If I were able, love,
to be with you eternally, if all things were
already lost. *Take then*
these songs I sang you,
north light, darkness, home, the ache
of the invisible and the pine trees
resinous with sunlight in the afternoon. O, the silence
in that naming, breaking
as you listened. And where the god stood inside you,
an empty shape, a wing.

ACCEPTING HEAVEN

And I who had never doubted
or believed, without understanding
how I had arrived: the stiff boughs along the avenues,
the lanes, wind-stirred, their blossoms white
against retreating cloud; the gravel
in the track, its bent bright grass;
and the peaks above the valley
chill pink in the afternoon ...

                                     enough sorrow
and it turns out there is nothing
that you cannot love. Maybe even knowing
it is done and elsewhere,
your old life, the rains
have finished. And the heart, bewildered,
filling with a cold spring light.

ENVOY: SEVEN VARIATIONS

I

And so I lay, waiting: a single flame felting the darkness.
Dawn, they tell us, breaks. It breaks.

Your voice came into me, then, like music. My lips,
your brow, your temple: how you called me

to the edge of myself.
Did I choose? I chose.

Sharp flutter in the feral trees: your voice
lifting in me like the wind, your touch

breaking through me like rain,
like sunlight. And the rain

falling in the silence behind the broken wind. O river
of kisses. O dance of the heart on the skin.

11

The damp night of spring, air
shimmering at dusk. Your eyes

have closed: we lie now
in the planet's palm.

Trellised by the porch, the rose nods,
drowsy with its own scent, dreaming and dreaming

of the sea. And you?
The storms we have ridden, have been ridden by.

O, but the sea wanders everywhere: the cool drift of it
through the darkening window. I lift

my head, mouth to your mouth, and taste
my own salt taste.

III

The earth's great arm
turns as it reaches into us. We are

the swirl of wing and fluke, the single thought
that moves like wind under the sea.

Your hands around me,
pulling deeper, the planet

torquing through us, your hair
like silk under my chin: your lips. This is

what I was made for.
I would be

the silver twist of fishes, the cloud-mind
of birds.

IV

I will not speak of this.
Let springtime come, the shoots that break like wavecrests in the dark.

This is my secret. No one, no one.
Poppyseed, as fine as sand, invisible on the raked earth.

I will lie down in silence. My own palm, just there. My ribs.
The humming underneath my window, lavender's blue scent.

Still, in those dreams, landscapes of snow, the road half-gone, black,
        narrowing with ice.
Does it matter? Be within me creature. Be without a voice.

Place your feet in darkness where your tracks cannot be seen.
What is furled, and furled, within.

Be mute, my body, silent, by the empty door.
Let springtime come.

v

Enter me and enter
me. Open me

to nothingness, make me
the nothing that I

really am. You are
its silence, and

the singing
of our emptiness.

What moves
inside that music is

the meaning of
what is.

VI

Languor. 2 a.m. The blown flower of your sex.
To kiss you, slowly

catch the satin of your underlip between my teeth.
To kiss you, your velvet weight on my tongue.

Stretched out along you, stretching under you,
the winding and unwinding of our names. To feel

earth's measure of us, true geometry, the pattern
spilling from the centre of the rose.

The cream silk of your inner arm, my hair caught on your nipple.
Pink-tipped, cream-white petals carpeting the porch.

My lips across the dark whorl in the centre of your chest.
The slight twitch of your thigh, wrapped under, over mine.

VII

Rain: the creeks in flood, lakes in the fields,
your mouth, your eyes, my hands on your skin:

we are learning to drown. Be breath. Be nothing.
At last, I am truly alive.

Leaves turning, autumn, each drop falling
a hundred times: desire empties me, and again

the music of your nakedness: that
silence. Here, now,

the final compass point,
the body dissolving in the soul:

my lips, your tongue, how even in this low light,
each thing gleams.

NOTES & ACKNOWLEDGEMENTS

A number of these poems were written to honour friends: "From Distant Lands" is for Barry Dempster, "Admetos" is for Jane Munro, and "Schumann: *Fantasie*, Op. 17" is for Bruce Vogt. While working on the manuscript, I have been deeply grateful for the fine editorial eyes of Sue Sinclair and Andrew Steeves and for the literary friendship of Karen Enns, Dexine Wallbank, and Tim Lilburn.

The epigraph to "Diotima to Hölderlin: A Remonstrance" is a remark Sokrates recalls that his teacher, Diotima, made to him when he was young. It might be translated: "How can you imagine you'll become accomplished in erotics if you don't know *that*?"

The italicized lines in "Schumann: *Fantasie*, Op. 17" are translations of lines from Beethoven's song cycle, "An die ferne Geliebte," Op. 98, on which Schumann based melodic material in the *Fantasie*. The original German texts were by Alois Jeitteles.

Versions of these poems have appeared in the following periodicals: *The Antigonish Review, Eleven Eleven, Event, The Fiddlehead, Focus, Grain, The Malahat Review, Poiesis, Vallum, The Walrus,* and *The Warwick Review*. "Autobiography" also appeared as a limited edition broadside from Greenboathouse Press, and "The Art of Fugue" was published as Vallum Chapbook Series No. 6. My sincere thanks to the editors and publishers involved.

My sincere thanks also to the BC Arts Council and the Canada Council for the Arts for their support during 2008 and 2010.

This book is for Robert Bringhurst.

Typeset in Deepdene by Andrew Steeves and printed offset and
bound under the direction of Gary Dunfield at Gaspereau Press,
Kentville, Nova Scotia. Deepdene was designed in 1927 by
Frederic Goudy and originally issued by Lanston Monotype.

7 6 5 4 3 2 1

National Library of Canada Cataloguing in Publication

Zwicky, Jan, 1955–
    Forge / Jan Zwicky.

Poems.
ISBN 978-1-55447-097-6

    I. Title.

PS8599.W53F67 2011   C811'.54   C2011-902125-0

GASPEREAU PRESS LIMITED
Gary Dunfield & Andrew Steeves ¶ Printers & Publishers
47 CHURCH AVENUE KENTVILLE NS B4N 2M7
WWW.GASPEREAU.COM